MEETING HOUSE ESSAYS

LIGHTING THE LITURGY

Viggo Bech Rambusch

Liturgy Training Publications

ACKNOWLEDGMENTS

Meeting House Essays was designed by Carolyn Riege and Kerry Perlmutter. It was typeset in Goudy Old Style by James Mellody-Pizzato. David Philippart was the editor, and Deborah Bogaert was the production editor. Cover photo by Antonio Pérez.

Other Meeting House Essays:

Number One: Sacred Places and the Pilgrimage of Life
Lawrence Hoffman

Number Two: Acoustics for Liturgy
A Collection of Articles of The Hymn Society in the United States and Canada

Number Three: Cherubim of Gold
Building Materials and Aesthetics
Peter E. Smith

Number Four: Places for Devotion
John Buscemi

Number Five: Renewing the City of God
The Reform of Catholic Architecture in the United States
Michael E. DeSanctis

Number Six: Iconography and Liturgy
Michael Jones-Frank

ISBN 1-56854-061-2

The entire parish huddles together, shivering and talking in quiet voices. It is midnight, yet no lights shine . . . it is pitch black. Then comes the sound of steel against flint as the kneeling minister attempts to strike a spark into a nest of wood shavings. Ten, fifteen times the flint is struck. Nothing. All is still dark. Finally, a spark jumps, and quickly, the minister leans down and blows softly into the nest, kindling a flame. The wood shavings catch fire and the minister adds small sticks, then larger ones, and finally full-sized logs. The new fire jumps and crackles to life. Another minister lights a waxed taper from the new fire and hands it to the pastor, who lights the paschal candle that the deacon holds. The new candle—a tall pillar of the finest wax—lifts the light of fire above the heads of those gathered.

Slowly the deacon with the candle leads the congregation away from the fire and toward the open doors of the darkened church. "Light of Christ," he sings, pausing before the door and holding the candle high. "Thanks be to God!" most sing in response. The procession moves slowly—all are taking tentative steps in the dark—up the aisle, following the flame. "Light of Christ," he intones again, in a slightly higher pitch. "Thanks be to God!" more respond. The deacon lowers the paschal candle and ministers light tapers from it. They pass, sharing the flame, through the people bunched together in disorganized ranks behind them. One by one faces are illuminated in the dark. Shadows dance on the ceiling and walls, pathways to seats become visible.

The deacon reaches the sanctuary. "Light of Christ," he sings once more at a still higher pitch. "Thanks be to God!" all

A flame from the paschal candle, divided but undimmed: The Easter Vigil begins with the Service of Light.

Photo: Regina Kuehn

respond, more heartily this time. He places the heavy candle into a large candlestick, and its flame flickers through clouds of perfumed smoke as the pastor swings the thurible toward it. Divided a hundred times, the flame is not diminished: All who are baptized stand holding its glow on the end of a taper. In place now, standing in the quiet light, the assembly looks at the deacon, who raises his voice to sing a lovely, ancient prayer that ends with the words:

> Accept this Easter candle,
>> a flame divided but undimmed,
>> a pillar of fire that glows to the honor of God.
> Let it mingle with the lights of heaven
>> and continue bravely burning
>> to dispel the darkness of this night!
> May the Morning Star which never sets find this
>> flame still burning;
>> Christ, that Morning Star, who came back from
>> the dead,
>> and shed his peaceful light on all people . . .

Thus begins the Easter Vigil, the most important liturgy of the Christian year. Recalling the very first act of creation itself, when God created light and separated day from night (Genesis 1:3), the service of light that begins the Vigil moves people by its primordial beauty. And not only at Easter. In some Christian communities, the light service begins evening prayer on Sundays, if not every day. And who has not been to a candlelight Christmas Eve service?

4

Even contemporary men and women—who, ironically, spend most if not all of their waking hours bathed in artificial light and are thus barely conscious of the rhythm of day and night—are still fascinated by the flicker of a candle flame at midnight, the interplay between light and darkness.

So naturally, light is a symbol of deity and a fundamental element in religious architecture. Like music and silence, like gesture and posture, light (and thus darkness) is integral to the religious experience. The sun in the temple, the torch in the catacomb, the candle in the cathedral—each has been used by religious people to proclaim something true about God and to praise God, the source of light.

Lighting the liturgy is thus as much about the poetry of light and darkness as it is about footcandles per square foot—an art as much as a science. Lighting a house of worship is a unique task because of the nature of what happens there.

In the Christian tradition, the parish church is a place where different actions take place at different times. A congregation acts in unison—processing or singing, for example. Particular ministers act for the sake of the whole—playing instruments or reading aloud, for example. And individuals come and engage in solitary actions—sitting or kneeling to pray, viewing or touching a cross, icon or statue, laying a bouquet of flowers, depositing money or goods for the poor, or lighting a candle in an otherwise darkened shrine. An important part of building a church is designing a system of lighting that takes into account such varied use as well as aids and reinforces the totality of actions that take place in the space.

This essay introduces the task of lighting the liturgy from the perspective of this variety of actions. It begins, however, by surveying what the scriptures say about light.

LIGHT IN HOLY SCRIPTURE

The Bible refers to light innumerable times. The first act of creation is the creation of light and its separation from darkness. On the third day, God created the "lights in the dome of the sky" (Genesis 1:14)—the sun, moon and stars. Both day and night are "ruled" by light, and the separation of light and darkness is judged by God to be good. Light—in varying degrees of brightness—is a gift from the Creator.

Light—and its antithesis, darkness or shadow—reveals and veils God's holy presence. When the Israelites leave Egypt, the book of Exodus says:

> The LORD went in front of them in a pillar of cloud
> by day, to lead them along the way, and in a pillar of

5

Natural light by day, candle-light by night creates a shrine that invites prayer. St. Mary Cathedral, San Francisco.

Photo: John Buscemi

fire by night, to give them light, so that they might travel by day and by night. Neither the pillar of cloud by day nor the pillar of fire by night left its place in front of the people. (Exodus 13:21–22)

The cloud (shadow, or darkness) and the fire (light) both reveal God's presence and at the same time veil it: The people know that God is near when they see the cloud or the fire, yet God is neither the cloud nor the fire. The divine fire lights the way. The divine cloud protects the Israelites from the Egyptians by wrapping them in darkness so that they can pass unnoticed and so that they can rest safely. (This should be a hint for lighting in churches: The modern eye, wearied by uniform fluorescent lighting in the workplace and marketplace, should be treated in the house of worship to light in varying degrees and to appropriately designed shadows.)

The psalmist sings of God's word as light: "Your word is a lamp to my feet, a light to my path" (Psalm 119:105). "Send me your light and your truth; let them lead me; let them bring me to your holy hill and to your dwelling" (Psalm 43:3). Even more so, the psalmist sings of God as light: "The LORD is my light and my salvation, whom should I fear?" (Psalm 27:1).

Isaiah not only uses light as a metaphor for God's glory ("Your light has come, and the glory of the LORD has risen upon you," Isaiah 60:1), but also uses it as a description of Jerusalem's mission ("Nations shall come to your light, and kings to the brightness of your dawn," Isaiah 60:3). God's people are to be a light in the world. Elsewhere, the prophets speak of knowledge of God and of wisdom as the light of life.

Jesus picks up this theme in numerous gospel passages. "You are the light of the world," Jesus says to the disciples in the Gospel of Matthew (5:14). "No one after lighting a lamp puts it under the bushel basket, but on the lampstand, and it gives light to all in the house. In the same way, let your light shine before others, so that they may see your good works and give glory to your Father in heaven" (5:15–16). And in the Gospel of John, Jesus says, "I am the light of the world. Whoever follows me will never walk in darkness but will have the light of life" (8:12).

In fact, the Gospel of John is full of references to light as a metaphor for Christ and his mission. In the 18 verses of his famous prologue, light is mentioned five times in reference to Christ and John the Baptist. The First Letter of John uses the image of light as a symbol of living a Christian life. And the Bible concludes with an image of the heavenly city in which the glory of God is light and Christ is the lamp:

> I saw no temple in the city, for its temple is the Lord God the Almighty and the Lamb. And the city has no need of sun or moon to shine on it, for the glory of God is its light, and its lamp is the Lamb. The nations will walk by its light, and kings of the earth shall bring their glory into it. Its gates will never be shut by day—and there will be no night there. (Revelation 21:22–25)

These and countless other scriptural references to light make it clear that light in a house of worship is more than a practical necessity. It is a powerful symbol of the presence and mystery of God, a sign of the church's mission on earth and an indication of what heaven is like. While liturgical lighting par excellence

Sunlight, when carefully accommodated by architecture, can illuminate the liturgy in significant ways. Above, the sun washes the ambo, where God's word is preached. Left, the sun illuminates the sacrificial meal and its ministers. St. Benedict the African Church, Chicago.

Photo: Antonio Pérez

is perhaps daylight first and candle flame second, electric illumination nonetheless plays a role in how light functions on a symbolic level.

CARING ABOUT LIGHTING

All knowledge comes to us through our five senses, especially seeing and hearing. Light determines what we see: Without it, we do not see, and by too much of it, we are blinded. We see an object the way it is lighted. Fall colors can be at their peak on a

The even lighting throughout the eucharistic hall unites the worshiping community and does not distinguish between sanctuary and assembly area. Our Lady of Grace Church, Edina, Minnesota.
Photo: Shin and Erich Koyama

hillside, but on a dull, overcast day, they are not exciting. On a bright, sunny day, though, they are vibrant—the sunlight gives the colors stunning intensity. So it is in a church. For a bride and groom to go to the altar in a dull church is a missed opportunity for beauty. The wedding clothes, the flowers, the faces of the collected family and friends all appear as autumn trees under an overcast sky. But in a well-lighted interior the flowers sing, the bride and groom are radiant, and the faces of friends and family reveal myriad emotions in light and shadow. Lighting makes the difference.

Next to music, nothing creates (or hinders the creation of) a supportive environment in which men and women congregate to praise and worship God as much as the lighting.

Yet lighting the liturgy is not simply about making things look pretty. How light is used often makes theological statements, too. What follows are two examples of why lighting systems in a house of worship need to be designed carefully, according to a good understanding of the liturgy that takes place there. These examples use information gathered and recommended by the group of professionals in North America most knowledgeable about lighting systems, the Illuminating Engineering Society (IES). The IES publishes booklets and articles on the subject and has made recommendations on light levels for various types of activities.

Light levels on vertical surfaces should be at a minimum ratio of 3:1 to draw the eye and provide good accents. St. Peter Cathedral, Erie, Pennsylvania.

Photo: Art Becker Photography

Skylights provide natural light. Talented architects make great use of natural light. Here, the assembly is well-lighted from above. Unity Temple, Oak Park, Illinois.

Photo: Martin V. Rambusch

Example one: Light level variations of less than 2 to 1 across a floor normally cannot be distinguished by the human eye. Therefore, if a pew area is lighted with from 10 to 20 footcandles (the basic unit of illumination) it is considered even lighting. However, many churches have lanterns that have a reflector lamp shooting down, giving a pool of light directly below. The light drops off between the lanterns, however, and creates shadowed areas of perhaps as much as 5 footcandles to one. This puts some people in the light and others quite noticeably in the shadows. The result is that when the people of God gather in that church, they are segregated by light and shadow. The goal is to be as one, to gather together. So light affects the gathering of the assembly.

If we add to this the fact that the sanctuary often is lighted at an even higher number of footcandles, not only is the congregation subdivided into sections of light and darkness, but as a whole it is separated from the altar and ambo. A "communion rail" of light is created.

Example two: In general, a change in light level of greater than 3 to 1 will draw the eye. Therefore, if we are trying to listen to a reading or a homily and the speaker is not lighted better than the immediate surroundings, it is not easy to focus on the speaker. If the vertical surface of the speaker's face and vestments were lighted at a level 3 times greater than that of the background, for example, we could see the speaker's face easily. Our eyes, which might wander, would be drawn back to the speaker simply by motor control, like a moth to a light bulb. And people who have difficulty hearing actually can comprehend more if they can see the speaker's face, expression, gestures—even unconsciously lip read. So light affects hearing, too.

In order to understand church lighting better, let us break the problem down into components and discuss each separately.

DAYLIGHTING

The first and most important component in church lighting is the flow of natural light into the building during daylight hours. As good architects did during earlier periods of Christian architecture—Byzantine, Gothic, Renaissance, Baroque—today's best architects pay attention to how light enters a building and where and how it falls. In fact, orienting church buildings so that their facades faced east and benefited from the morning sun was considered an important architectural requirement by the early Roman church.

Candlelight in a darkened shrine (background) and sunlight bathing a tomb (foreground): The careful use of light and shadow creates an environment of mystery conducive to liturgy. Church of St. Francis, Urbino, Italy.

Photo: Peter E. Smith

The bronze cross in this church in Cologne, Germany, is lit from the side and holds the light due to its polish.

Photo: Viggo Bech Rambusch

Adé Bethune, a noted designer and liturgical consultant, wrote convincingly in the Easter 1982 issue of *Sacred Signs* of the significance of daylight in church architecture:

> Foundations, walls and roof are the chief elements of architecture. Yet these solid elements only serve to define an open interior space, an empty volume experienced to some extent by walking about in it, but experienced especially through light and sound.
>
> In a church building, the invisible but illuminating presence of Christ, "the light of the world," cannot be more eloquently expressed than by a source of daylight pouring in from above (clerestory windows, dome windows, skylights) into the middle of the people. The Pantheon, Hagia Sophia and St. Peter Basilica's dome are prime examples, but so too are more modest buildings where the architect conceived light as the chief liberating factor. (16–17)

In constructing a new church, this is a specific consideration. For example, to build a wall of windows behind a sanctuary usually creates glare. Glare makes it difficult to see, especially for older people; the opening and closing of the iris of the eye slows down and peripheral vision deteriorates in people over 55 years of age. So an elderly person trying to see the presider in a church with an altar in front of a window automatically has a problem looking there, perhaps even to the point of physical discomfort.

A light-conscious architect will use devices like skylights to draw attention to the baptistry, the sanctuary, the tabernacle in the reservation chapel or particular works of art. In sunny climates, skylights sometimes have adjustable shutters to control the amount of light and maintain the proper range of contrasts.

Great architects such as Eliel Saarinen and Frank Lloyd Wright did wonderful things with light—much like the Arab architects of 1000 years ago. Wright created a device called a light shelf to bounce light up onto the ceiling. Saarinen, at The Massachusetts Institute of Technology, surrounded his chapel building with a reflecting pool and had low, "eyebrow" windows at the bottom of the chapel walls to let in a most interesting, general ambient light. There were no regular windows as such. But he included a skylight over the altar and commissioned a mobile of small round glass disks, arranged like a tree with branches, to hang beneath the skylight and behind the altar to reflect daylight.

So part of the architect's job and the building commission's responsibility is to see that daylight is admitted both to help the

Stained glass beautifully filters light into the interior. St. Ignatius Cathedral, Palm Beach Gardens, Florida.

Photo: Harold Seckinger

congregation when it gathers for liturgy as well as to support the private devotional prayer of individuals at other times.

STAINED GLASS

Of great importance is the natural light transformed and admitted by stained-glass windows. The windows act as huge color gelatins tempering the light and creating a setting psychologically supportive of worship. For many people, stained glass "makes" a church a sacred place.

Stained-glass windows function on four levels. First, like any windows, stained-glass windows are an integral part of the building, sealing out the weather and helping to maintain an established, controlled environment.

Second, they fragment the opening in the wall, reducing the scale of a large opening by filling it with a multitude of small pieces of glass. In Moor architecture, for example, the artist absorbs the viewer into infinity by so arranging the design that one becomes mesmerized, much like what happens when one stands at the rear of a ship looking at the wake of the boat as it moves across the water.

Third, the choice of colors for the glass affects the quality of the interior light. The glass warms the light or cools it, for example, by giving splashes of red or blue on the walls or floor on a bright day.

Fourth, when stained-glass windows have figures, they function as part of the iconographic program of the interior. This function has little to do with issues of lighting, although figures that are only faintingly discernible due to a lack of light may end up being distracting.

The artificial lighting of stained glass is never completely satisfactory. To be viewed at its best, stained glass needs ever-changing daylight. Bright sunlight reads at 10,000 footcandles on a light meter, yet only about 50–100 footcandles on average are delivered to the interior of the church through stained glass. Achieving this through artificial lighting is tricky. It is aesthetically essential to not see the lamps outside through the window. This is less of a problem with heavily painted windows or with chipped glass fenestration. Clear glass windows need a scrim cloth, a curtain between the lights and the window to diffuse the light and help the viewer read the window legibly. Gas discharge lamps are not always best—monochromatic light washes out the window's colors.

ARTIFICIAL LIGHTING

Given the witness of scripture, natural light should be the principal force for illuminating the liturgy. Artificial light—electric illumination—is best considered as a supplement to the natural light except, of course, at night or on days when the weather is dark and gloomy. (Liturgy is celebrated now at night more often than it ever was. Parishes with churches that were built before the Second Vatican Council gave permission for evening Masses should evaluate their lighting system with this in mind.)

Artificial lighting is at its best if it is worked into the architecture of a building's interior in such a way that one is not conscious of where the light is coming from. In this way lighting complements the architecture and focuses attention on the action of the liturgy rather than on its source.

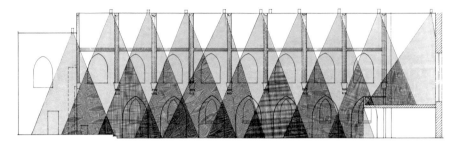

Recessed downlights are located in an accessible attic. Overlapping provides even lighting in the room. This plan is for Sacred Hea Church, Winnetka, Illinois.

Photo: Rambusch Lighting

Lanterns must have very low wattage or else they become a source of glare. Lanterns are decorative, but alone cannot provide all the necessary light. Sacred Heart Cathedral, Richmond, Virginia.

Photo: Katherine Wetzel

There are four main functions artificial lighting serves: lighting specific tasks, lighting the best architectural features of the building, lighting vertical surfaces for accent, and lighting for special effect.

1. *Lighting the specific tasks* performed during public worship, such as greeting one another, processing, reading and singing. This calls first for good horizontal surface light—on the people, the hymnal, the sacramentary, the lectionary and the floor. This light should be adequate, diffuse and shadow-free. It is most easily and economically generated from above by means of downlights. The higher the units are, the fewer that are needed; the more overlapping of light beams, the better. Of course, maintenance is a factor. If there is a catwalk above, one only needs access to the catwalk. Otherwise, lowering devices are called for—or a maintenance electrician with a lift coming in on a schedule, perhaps once every two years for a group relamping.

The alternatives are less satisfactory. Indirect lighting puts the congregation in shadows. In most churches, one would have to deliver to the ceiling three times the amount of light actually needed, assuming a reflective ceiling, in order to cast sufficient light on the reading surface. So for 15 footcandles on a missal, fixtures would have to deliver 45 footcandles to the ceiling. This creates a bright ceiling and puts the congregation in shadows. If the ceiling is dark or richly molded, then it is impossible to get a significant amount of light down.

Lantern fixtures either must be used in great profusion or have the bulb at the bottom of the cylinder, which creates glare. (It is no different from hanging bare bulbs.) Lanterns were great as a replacement for gaslights 70 years ago when 2 footcandles was considered good illumination. But today, they are more for decoration (see number 4).

The Illuminating Engineering Society, which is under pressure from the U.S. government to improve energy conservation, has lowered its recommended light levels for a church from the standards of the 1960s. Where it was recommended in the 1960s to have 15 to 40 footcandles, today the IES recommends a base level in the nave of 10 to 20 footcandles. There is an exception—where the congregation is predominately elderly (over 55), the levels can be doubled.

The best type of bulb for lighting the liturgy is the tungsten-halogen. It is the most efficient, longest-lasting and best color-rendering incandescent source available today. All discharge lamps (fluorescent and high intensity discharge types, such as mercury, halide or high pressure sodium) involve ballasts and are expensive to dim. They only dim partially—from perhaps

100 percent to 20 percent—and then go off when the arc collapses. Being unable to dim the lights in a church is a disadvantage now that evening liturgy is more frequent. It's good to be able to dim the lights for evening celebrations.

Because the burning hours of the fixtures in a place for worship are so low—10 to 20 hours a week—there are other considerations besides initial lumen output that are more important. One is the quality of the light. It is better to achieve a continuous spectrum, like sunlight, than to bathe the interior in a yellowish or bluish cast. Another problem with discharge lamps is ballast noise, especially as the system ages.

Discharge lamps also must cool for a while after they are turned off before they can go on again. And when they go on, sometimes they flicker for several minutes. This would be very disruptive of the beginning of the Easter Vigil or a vespers service, when a few lights may be on as people gather, they are turned off to begin the liturgy in darkness, and then are soon turned back on to assist with reading.

A parish would exercise the best stewardship by initially buying the best equipment it can afford. Then it will only have to relight once a generation—once every 33 years.

2. *Lighting the best architectural features*, be they ceilings, walls or special elements. This takes sensitive study: A wash of light can be thrown on a wall. A timber ceiling and vaults can be cross-lighted. Artistically, lighting a reredos can be an exciting challenge. Grazing light—not too severe—can reveal a sculpture with highlights and shadows that bring out the beauty of the piece. Apses can be illuminated, but however that might be achieved, there should be some general ambient light. The recommended level is perhaps ¼ to ⅓ of the task lighting (the reading light in the pews, for example). If this is not achieved, then the space becomes dark, gloomy, shadowed and uninteresting. If there is no discreet method of achieving general ambient light, then here is an opportunity for typical church lanterns as long as they do not create glare. Remember, the surface of the lantern's cylinder should not be brighter than the people and objects being viewed—during the homily, for example, the face of the speaker should be brighter than the lantern.

Architectural lighting greatly contributes to the aesthetics of the setting, helping to create the best environment for worship. If the opportunity for lighting worthy architectural features is missed, then the interior feels dull, harsh, inhospitable and incapable of evoking a sense of mystery.

3. *Accent lighting*. Here we are lighting vertical surfaces—the altar, the face of the preacher in the ambo, the cantor's stand,

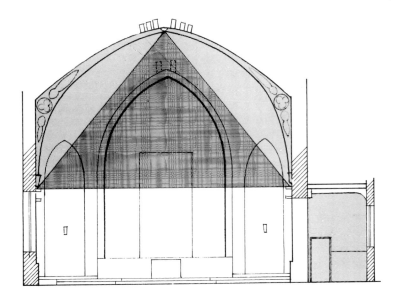

Urns mounted on the capital columns cross-light the vault. Sacred Heart Church, Winnetka, Illinois

Photo: Rambusch Lighting

Architectural lighting illuminates the reredos and the fresco on the east wall. Christ Church Episcopal, Cranbrook, Michigan.

Photo: Jack Kausch

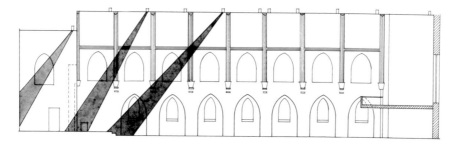

Accent lighting emphasizes various points of action: the front of the middle aisle, the altar, the ambo. The light fixtures should be at a 45° angle and located to the right and left of the point being illuminated. Sacred Heart Church, Winnetka, Illinois.

Photo: Rambusch Lighting

Accent lighting can emphasize a work of art or an object of devotion. St. Peter Cathedral, Erie, Pennsylvania.

Photo: Art Becker

Architectural lighting can illuminate a building's special feature, such as these carved and gilded capitals. St. Peter Cathedral, Erie, Pennsylvania.

Photo: Art Becker

the communion stations, the place where the bride and the groom stand, the door of the tabernacle in the reservation chapel, an icon or a sculpture in a niche—whatever is a visual focus of attention in a given situation. The light can come from the right and the left, perhaps from a 50-degree angle with the light from the south stronger and the light from the north softer, to give character and interest. The level of such lighting should be about three times the level of the reading light.

4. Finally, there is *special-effect lighting*. This gives sparkle and highlight to certain objects during certain liturgies. Foci would include polished metal candlesticks, the procession cross or a significant work of art that is the focus of devotion. Illuminating such items can be achieved in other ways, also—gold leaf on the bevels and chamfers of the woodwork, or highlights in the lanterns, for example.

Lit from within and without, the ambry shines as a repository of the holy oils. St. Peter Cathedral, Erie, Pennsylvania.

Photo: Art Becker

A LIGHTING SYSTEM

Understanding the four specific functions that lighting plays, next it is important to see how the lighting designer can create different settings depending on parish usage.

First, a modern dimmer can have several preset buttons that will create different lighting arrangements for different events. For example:

1. Visiting hours setting. The church is open, no corporate worship is scheduled, and people come only to pray. Lights are focused on significant pieces of devotional art and lights in the blessed sacrament chapel would be on.

2. Pre- and post-liturgy setting. Lighting for the 20 minutes or so before and after Mass, as people are entering or dispersing.

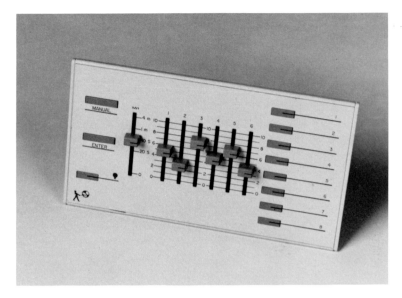

A dimming panel provides preset lighting combinations that can be activated with the push of a button.

Photo: Strand Lighting

3. Daily Mass, small funeral or wedding setting. Only those sections of the church necessary for the number of people gathered are lit.

4. Sunday Mass setting. The whole interior is lit.

5. Evening setting. For those services (Saturday evening Mass, vespers, some weddings, penance liturgies) that begin in semi-darkness, high architectural lighting and accent lighting is used, as well as low task lighting.

6. Choir practice setting. Only the music area is illuminated.

7. Manual control setting. This allows for maximum flexibility in casting the entire room in darkness and then gradually lighting it as the liturgy progresses, as for the Easter Vigil or Christmas midnight Mass, for example.

8. Maintenance setting. Downlights only.

Second, each of the four functions will be divided into channels. For example:

Task lighting
1. Sanctuary
2. Nave forward
3. Nave rear and side aisles
4. Music area

Architectural lighting
5. Apse
6. Ceiling
7. Column capitals

Accent lighting
8. Altar
9. Ambo

Accent lighting cont'd.	10. Font
	11. Devotional: tabernacle and statues
Festive lighting	12. Lanterns

The control preset means that the light levels of these 12 groups of lights in a large church will go to a pre-determined level when used. For example, in the pre- and post-liturgy setting, the architectural lighting can be on full (90 percent); the devotional lighting and accent on the font (people use it to bless themselves as they enter) can be on full (90 percent); the accent lighting on the altar and ambo can be off; the lanterns can be on full (90 percent); and the task lighting can be on 30 percent.

During the opening song, the devotional lighting goes off—to 0 percent—and the architectural lighting and lanterns go down to 30 percent. The accent lighting on the ambo and the altar, and the task lighting, go up to full—90 percent. This change in lighting happens subtly during the opening song and procession, thus not drawing attention to itself.

Note that 90 percent—not 100 percent—is considered full. This also means seriously extended lamp life, and the gradual fades in a dimmer—"on" to "off"—are more gentle to the lamp filament than a sudden switching on.

The location for the controls for the dimmer should be carefully thought out. The main control should be located at a position from which the entire church can be viewed, but then it must be kept under lock and key. There can be several locations for the remote preset button control. For example: one in the sacristy, another by the organ console and a third located conveniently for the head usher.

THE PARISH LAMP LIGHTER

While the lighting system is not as involved, complicated, expensive or hard to maintain as the organ, it still needs attention—and on special occasions such as the Paschal Triduum or Christmas Eve, it could use an operator if there is a control board. Here then is an opportunity for someone in the parish to assist with the liturgy, much as sacristans, eucharistic ministers, lectors, servers, ushers and choir members do. A parish could designate someone to be responsible for the proper maintenance of the system and to be familiar with its operation. Maybe this is the sacristan or the head usher, or maybe it is another person. Every church building is different, and every congregation has its special character. But a person working in conjunction with the clergy, music minister and congregation

Church entrances should be illuminated to extend welcome. Significant architecture illuminated at night can help the church literally be a neighborhood beacon. St. Mary Cathedral, San Francisco.

Photo: Courtesy of the Cathedral

can create specific light settings that will support the activity in the given space at various times.

EMERGENCY LIGHTING AND ILLUMINATED SIGNS

This essay's primary concern is the proper lighting of the liturgy. One other aspect of interior lighting that affects churches is emergency lighting and illuminated exit signs. Emergency lighting is defined as lighting designed to supply illumination essential to safety of life and property in the event of a failure of the normal supply. A parish must know the local building codes to which it is subject; these will determine the kind and location of any required emergency lighting.

Illuminated exit signs can disrupt a church interior. When required, they should be planned for at the same time finishes and fixtures are chosen. Such signs must be clearly visible, of course, but perhaps fixtures that harmonize with other interior elements could be chosen or even designed so that a typical, industrial "EXIT" sign does not garishly float above a beautifully carved baptistry door, for example.

EXTERIOR LIGHTING

Here are a few general principles about lighting the exterior of the church building:

1. The entrances to the church should be so illuminated at night as to be inviting and welcoming. The doors and threshold should be well lighted with a wash of light on the doors and a general glow of light throughout the area. The walkway from the sidewalk across the terrace, if there is one, should have landscape lighting (perhaps from bollards—that is, posts). The lighting of the entrance can be accomplished by fixtures attached to brackets and/or by standards.

2. It is a good idea to provide an illuminated sign identifying the church by name and giving a schedule of liturgies and special events as well as the names of the people involved. This should be so placed that it can be easily read from the sidewalk.

3. Perhaps the most significant architectural element in a parish church is its steeple or tower. This can be lighted by floodlights properly located on two, three or four sides so that it reads as a three-dimensional sculptured element and not just a flat surface.

4. Some churches have particularly interesting architectural characteristics, like a facade, for instance. Floodlighting elements such as these may increase people's appreciation of the building and pique their interest in the parish. It may also allow the parish to be a good neighbor by providing some night lighting in the area. Care must be taken when lighting the facade, however, so that the lighting does not trespass into people's windows and cause problems.

5. In conjunction with the possibility of floodlighting the facade, a major stained-glass window can be lighted from the inside as a way of sharing it with the neighborhood. Care should be taken so that the fixtures do not detract from the view of the window from the inside and to ensure that they are not visible through the window when viewed from the outside. An intermediate element such as a scrim curtain may be needed to diffuse the light so that the interior fixtures are not seen from the street.

Light of Christ, shine forth
in the Church! Santa
Maria di Castello Church,
Tarquinia, Italy.
Photo: Peter E. Smith

6. Church parking lot lighting is like any commercial parking lot lighting, and standards are provided by the lighting fixture industry. However, for church lots, thought might also be given to the occasional church fairs or social functions that are sometimes held there. A few power lines that could supply power to booths and other outlets needed during such activities might be run to the base of the parking lot standards.

7. Shrines or pieces of outdoor sculpture located on the church grounds should be lighted. Perhaps two floodlights (one to the right and one to the left) powered by an underground conduit and hidden in shrubbery would work well.

All exterior lighting should be thought of as a unified and total lighting composition and should be so coordinated that the total effect is pleasant and attractive. It should be on timers so that it goes on after sunset and goes off at a determined time

(11:00 PM, for example). Such timers will need to be adjusted according to the seasons of the year in order to avoid unnecessary power consumption. Regular, periodic cleaning of outdoor fixtures is also necessary.

SHINE WITH THE LIGHT OF GOD'S SPLENDOR

In the *Rite of Dedication of a Church and an Altar*, the church building is sprinkled with water, anointed with chrism and filled with incense. Then the altar is dressed with a white cloth and the bishop gives the deacon a lighted candle, saying these words:

> Light of Christ,
> shine forth in the church
> and bring all nations
> to the fullness of truth.

Then the deacon lights the candles that surround the altar for the first time—they were not lit before Mass, and no candles were carried in procession. Then all the candles and lamps in the church are lit, including the twelve candles that mark the twelve places where the walls were anointed with chrism. A song is sung during this ritual, the second verse of which proclaims:

> Jerusalem, city of God,
> you will shine with the light of God's splendor.

The science and the art of lighting the liturgy is an opportunity to use light—the first thing ever created—to give God praise and transform our earthly communities into beacons that point heavenward. Let us not miss this opportunity.

FOR FURTHER REFLECTION

In the beginning when God created the heavens and the earth, the earth was a formless void and darkness covered the face of the deep, while a wind from God swept over the face of the waters. Then God said "Let there be light"; and there was light. And God saw that the light was good; and God separated the light from the darkness. God called the light "day" and the darkness "night." And there was evening and there was morning, the first day.

Genesis 1:1–5

And God said, "Let there be lights in the dome of the sky to separate the day from the night; and let them be for signs and for seasons and for days and for years, and let them be lights in the dome of the sky to give light upon the earth." And so it was. God made the two great lights—the greater light to rule the day and the lesser light to rule the night—and the stars. God set them in the dome of the sky to give light upon the earth, to rule over the day and over the night, and to separate the light from the darkness. And God saw that it was good. And there was evening and there was morning, the fourth day.

Genesis 1:14

We praise and thank you, O God,
through your son Jesus Christ our Lord,
through whom you have enlightened us
by revealing the light that never fades.
Joy to all creatures, honor, feasting and delight!
Night is falling and day's allotted span draws to a close.
We have enjoyed your gift of daylight;
brighten now our evening hours.

Evening thanksgiving based
on the Apostolic Tradition

O send out your light and your truth; let them lead me;
let them bring me to your holy hill and to your dwelling.
Then I will go to the altar of God, to God my exceeding joy;
and I will praise you with the harp, O God, my God.

Psalm 43:3–4

O radiant light, O sun divine
Of God the Father's deathless face,
O image of the light sublime
Phos Hilaron   That fills the heav'nly dwelling place.

John 8:12   Again Jesus spoke to them, saying "I am the light of the world."

Christ our Light!
The Roman Rite   Thanks be to God!

Accept this Easter candle,
    a flame divided, but undimmed,
    a pillar of fire that glows to the honor of God.
Let it mingle with the lights of heaven
    and continue burning bravely
    to dispel the darkness of this night!
May the Morning Star which never sets
    find this flame still burning:
    Christ, that Morning Star, who came back from the dead,
    and shed his peaceful light on all people,
    your Son who lives and reigns for ever and ever.
Exsultet, The Roman Rite   Amen.

Jesus said to them, "You are the light of the world. A city built on a hill cannot be hid. No one after lighting a lamp puts it under a bushel basket, but on the lampstand, and it gives light to all in the house. In the same way let your light shine before others, so that they may see your good works and give glory to
Matthew 5:14   your Father in heaven."

We believe in you, Lord Jesus Christ.
Fill our hearts with your radiance
and make us the children of light!

Rite of Christian Initiation of
Adults, The Roman Rite

Then the bishop gives to the deacon a lighted candle, and says:
Light of Christ,
shine forth in the Church
and bring all nations
to the fulness of truth.

Then the bishop sits. The deacon goes to the altar and lights the candles for the celebration of the eucharist. Then the festive lighting takes place: all the candles, including those at the places where the anointings were made, and the other lamps are lit as sign of rejoicing. Meanwhile the following antiphon is sung with the canticle of Tobias:

The Dedication of a
Church and of an Altar,
The Roman Rite

Your light will come, Jerusalem; upon you the glory of the Lord will dawn and all nations will walk in your light, alleluia!

A great portent appeared in heaven: a woman clothed with the sun, with the moon under her feet, and on her head a crown of twelve stars.

Revelation 12: 1

I saw no temple in the city, for its temple is the Lord God the Almighty and the Lamb. And the city has no need of sun or moon to shine on it, for the glory of God is its light, and its lamp is the Lamb.

Revelation 21:22

SOURCES

All scriptures citations are taken from the New Revised Standard Version Bible, copyright 1989, Division of Christian Education of the National Council of Churches of Christ in the United States of America.

We praise and thank you . . .
Excerpt from *Praise God in Song: Ecumenical Daily Prayer*, ed. John Allyn Melloh, William G. Storey (Chicago: GIA Publications, Inc., 1979).

Christ our Light . . .
Excerpt from *The Sacramentary*. English translation prepared by the International Commission on English in the Liturgy, copyright 1973.

Accept this Easter candle . . .
Excerpt from *The Sacramentary*. English translation prepared by the International Commission on English in the Liturgy, copyright 1973.

We believe in you . . .
Excerpt from *Rite of Christian Initiation of Adults*. English translation prepared by the International Commission on English in the Liturgy, copyright 1981.

Then the bishop gives the deacon . . .
Excerpt from *Dedication of a Church and an Altar*. English translation prepared by the International Commission on English in the Liturgy, copyright 1977.